THE MENDER

poems by hannah dulaney

Copyright © 2024 by Hannah Dulaney

First Edition

Cover design and interior layout by Matthew J. Distefano
Cover image by Edward Munsch and is in the Public Domain

Print ISBN 978-1-964252-22-3
Electronic ISBN 978-1-964252-27-8
Printed in the United States of America

Published by Quoir
Chico, California
www.quoir.com

for Richard
who sees

CONTENTS

For when I fall into the abyss,
I go straight into it,
head down and heels up,
and I'm even pleased
that I'm falling
in such a humiliating position.
For me, I find it beautiful.
And so in that very shame
I suddenly begin
a hymn.

FYODOR DOSTOEVSKY

Part I

I have this image
stuck deep down in me
like a crow bar
between my throat and kidney:
There's a swimming pool
and we're all in it and
we're floating
but not on water.
We're holding tightly to
the rafts that are one another,
and no one is drowning.

The Bargain

You never knew your mother
at a time when she was not your mother
at a time when you had not bargained with her blood.

You never knew your father
at a time when he was not your father
at a time when you had not been caught in his hands.

And after all these years,
I don't much care for what the attachment theorists have to say.

Praise the bleeding,
though you are less,
you will become more.

Praise the fire,
as it licks your palms
you will not be burned.

And above all,
praise the miracle of needing,
for you may soon be needed.

Talking to Roadkill

I am a terrible person,
headless raccoon.

I am bad at my job,
headless raccoon.

I am always a little smelly,
headless raccoon.

I have been alone for 24 years,
headless raccoon.

And, yes,
your body is all wrong now,
and your guts may be a broken jam jar too evenly spread across Holgate and 28th
at the hands of a tire knife,
but, roadkill,
at least you didn't see it coming.

Man's Man is so 1896

So instead, I say
that's a real *flower's flower*,
Blessed be the *rose's rose.*
She's a real *mother's mother.*
Girl's girl is too obvious, try
woman's woman for a real splash
if you know what I mean. The
North Sea is the *ocean's ocean,*
and this caramelized onion dip is
a true *spread's spread.* You've
travelled far. You're a *traveller's
traveller* and I want you here in
this *home's home* with the *light's light* so
dim and buzzing with beer. You
have a real *nose's nose*, did you know?
Something to think about. "A nose
you can really get behind," my
teacher's teacher used to say.
What's keeping us this close? What's
moving your hand? Did you know?
I need to possess *someone's someone.*

The Origins of Labor

one a laughing house with cathedral attendance
spare   room for the dunce and his dancer's figure called womanly
spare   pointed calves crested like waves or valley things move tall
spare   children born death washing their heads

write me into sacred text as one
coy and humble no
different from belly fat in
hip swung lambs rearing late

had we been less vain
spare   for the aching skulls that throbbed to night voices
spare   for the hollow snap of turtle backs found just in pond
spare   mosaic beatles under rocky dorm

if I fail to become scripture, house, or lamb
must I keep my labor?

Wrong Reading

I begin a hymn,
I become the hymn

I fall silent
I become the silence

I begin to run
I become the running

One Year Married

You eat baby back ribs as if you're holding up a doubting nun's crucifix,
shrouded in Stubb's Smokey Mesquite rather than habit,
electing to indulge only in carnivorous dopamine,
as to only make love with venial sin,
but it occurs to me now that murder should be classified, if anything, as carnivorous.

It makes me wonder where you learned that kind of fear.

I want to speak to you in child's rhymes,
so you never have to guess at what I'll say next,
and I'd rather the galaxy spill her milky secrets from her breasts
than see you wash your hands of her blood,
and, in doing so, your inheritance.

I've never been allowed to cleanse like that.

The closest I came was doggy paddling in a borrowed infinity pool
that looked nothing like Bethesda,
or how I've always imagined it to look,
as infinity overlooked brown hills and brown cows,
their sleepy shadows waxed alongside the moon's.

I walked away holier, wishing someone I loved would have told me I looked it.

Instructions

I can't recall
if we've ever touched,
but we've been living
far too long
off of lingering looks
and instructions
on how to use the washing machine.

Migratory

Four nights after the full moon,
we sank:
into the pool, under the cover
of bats mistaking us for bugs
and shooting stars you could
never catch. You crawled on
your beautiful belly, your
chin touching the water, and
I told you you looked like a
salamander. You also looked
like a pile of rocks I
might drive by on a road trip,
a cluster of bees, a throw blanket,
a letter with no return address.

I couldn't bring myself
to touch myself
after we spoke of babies,
hookups, and New Mexico,
my laughter floating
above us into the steam.
I'd gotten used
to the habit of pulling our words down
into the folds of me
and further toward
the places I wish you were.

That night I let every letter lie,
falling asleep remembering
how you told me in your softest voice
that there is one
kind of red salamander

who migrates from Mexico
to California every year.
"You think of him as a still thing,
but he probably walks at
least a mile a day."

My Friend Grows Tomatoes Because She Knows They are God

My friend grows tomatoes because she knows they are God.
A *kind of sexuality* she tells me, then
asks if I've ever gotten turned on from lying in the sun.

How do I respond
to such a holy question?

How does anyone respond to holiness?

The Love Mirror

To look would be to die certain of many things.
In brief,
to look would be to die.

The moss and the thicket crowning
your watery head, the movement of it
confusing your hair with itself, is it all
what it seems?

Again, I ask, can you let yourself be loved?

Just as birds choose to fly in the shape of birds—
give yourself permission to look,
even if only the once.

Deluged

For Marlys

The woman at the secondhand store
asks her sister if Debbie's been around;
the fourth Debbie I've heard mentioned
in the last two weeks, and it gets me
thinking about these strangers
whose names are kept safe
in the mouths of their friends,
and then about the child who says
without speaking, "I see you,"
to a rock he puts in his pocket,
and the way I notice one of my hairs
transubstantiate into the perfect
letter Q on the surface of my
bathwater, and when I tell Gianna
she's a whisperer as she sits
holding the dog's head in her lap
and he lets her, she doesn't look up,
only nods, in perfect agreement.

Face the Facts

The damage is a guarantee.
So, may you break wholly,
may you forgive graciously,
and know, you can always
send your pieces back to me.

Our Lot

Lately I've been thinking about our lot
and what it means to go to the places
we don't always want to go. I'm trying
to remind myself that desire isn't a sign I'm unfulfilled.
I'm trying to remind myself of the monk
whose name I've since forgotten, the one
who did all the dishes as a way to prove to himself
good can be mundane can be good.
What if our lot is to move our bodies in such a way
that the starlings see us and blow out of their trees like a geyser?
What if our lot is to stare at a whole head of roasted elephant garlic
with eyes the size of dinner plates
knowing it will soon be devoured,
and not only devoured,
but tasted?

Anticipatory

The day after you nearly died
I made beef stroganoff at 11 am
and, later in the afternoon,
burnt my hand on the steam
when I took the leftovers out
of the microwave.

The next day: breakfast, lunch, and dinner.
Beef stroganoff.

All day long, beef stroganoff.

I didn't want anything else. I felt sick.
I felt like I needed more distractions.
Convinced myself
salt, cream, and stewed meat
would replace the place of the bloodied
image of you.

Yes, I became beef stroganoff's whore.
There are worse ways to grieve.

Our dalliance lasted until news of you
returned. I romanced your almost-death
between slurps of egg noodle (it was
all I had in the cupboard) and ground
grass-fed beef (it was all I had in the freezer).

Thinking, if only this were 1900, the year
your father was born, maybe I'd hear
the news a little slower and believe you were
alive a little longer and have no idea what a

carotid artery was. Certainly, I would have blamed your ailments on
the devil or at least spelled the word "lymfnodes" right.

We were unlucky enough to be alive this year.
And here I am, stuffing my carotid artery with
a little more animal fat. Sprinkling dehydrated
cheese over eight layers of dairy, imagining
what I'll tell people when you're gone.

God, why can't I grieve like a skinny person?
God, why can't I stop grieving while you're alive?

Part II

No one is drowning,
and it's not because
there is no water, but
because we're all smushed
in there just right
nicely layered like
tiramisu. And it's hot,
but not uncomfortably so.
We're just warming
each other
with the suns
that are our bodies.

Question

Do you think when someone,
a woman,
maybe,
gets hit by a car and
is killed
instantly
on her short walk from home
that God closes his eyes
or hits the fast forward button
and howls in his slippers
"I can't watch this part!"

The Mender

For Richard

What does it say about us?
This distance
born of a closeness gone wrong.

My mother calls it a communication issue.

Now's a good time to confess
that while you've been dying,
I've been tasting

bottles of wine and cinnamon sticks,
sweat on my upper lip,
the necks of men,
birthday cake and loneliness
disguised as the holy.

I ran to the arms of the mountain I knew would hold me (another confession),
and I heard your new voice for the first time.
There was no other place I wanted to learn
that someone I once loved was going to die.

"Will He do a miracle?" You asked.
But all I could make out was
"Will this be the time He restrains himself?"

In a bed a thousand miles away from me
my friend's lover tells her he believes
there are parts of us even God doesn't touch.

Methods

this mouth drowns itself,
eats itself. recognizes
something growing and shaking,
something shining,
something kind and deadly
moving through the fibrous hand,
splitting where it can,
taking root in the stockpile,
finding footing, then nothing,
then bed, the rock bed. it
feasts on minerals, still grows,
settles down, won't move,
protrudes, protracts, snaps back,
spills over the sides until the
bath floats to the top soaked
in sweet sinewed fertilizer,
sprouting nippling buds.
to move beyond the marbled skin,
to coil oneself around the feet,
to sanitize every side with pecking kisses.
oh, the mess we've made!

Funeral

Spare the grudge against yourself
and quit your thinking
that just because we die
any moment spent in unkindness is a sin.

I don't say it often, but in this, you're simply wrong.
You are allowed to live a life stained in glass,
but if you choose to plant your feet in a crack of concrete
it's just as well.

Or perhaps you need the grudge
to hold when your hands are empty;
a new play thing, your heart-shaped box.
I cannot tell you what to do or what is best.

I only know our time is rippling,
and it's alright if you get it all wrong.

God's Other Lovers

Much like everything else
you thought you were the first.
Spent your days pretending
like zinnias, cedar smoke,
and the emotional machinations
of the triangle didn't exist.
Had you convinced yourself
you have more charisma
than a rhino's horn? More pull
than the ocean's undertow?
Do you speak the northern
pacific dialect of the five
orca pod, each echo a different
way of saying 'yes'?
And while your big toe is
enticing, and your ear lobe
its own mystery, I can't
promise you a spot on this list.
Most are surprised to learn
that a prayer is nothing more
than a flirtation.
Nothing less either.

The Servant

Do not hold me to it.
Do not hold me to what
I cannot say
as though it were my choice
to remain in this cold house
as the servant
of many silences.

Sometimes I Can't Stand Poetry

I know
and you know
poetry to be as vital
as air, pushing
blood through the heart,
a force
rarely at rest, so,
please,
when you can,
leave the subliminals behind.
The hungry
do not need another metaphor,
the thirsty
do not need another river
from which no man can drink.

Eyespot (Mimicry)

Let the lover be disgraceful, crazy, absentminded.
Someone sober will worry about things going badly.
Let the lover be.

— **RUMI**

You moved, then I moved,
under the city and out,
close as we could get to
the circumference of Friday night.

Following your bravery,
tormented by your body's length,
we watched as twenty three plates fell onto the floor,
and I knew I loved you when I was jealous.

In turn,
you reached out and stroked my solitude,
you told me it had been good to me, then
you asked me to take it to auction.
So I did.

For weeks I caught myself there
singing in the dark, worshipping
the signs—
did you pray too?
For another night like the
one we spent:
fingers in each other's ears,
your voice stepping on my neck,
the gray couch, the lonely together—
how many times did I dream it?

Sometimes, a Cave

I don't know where these years are coming from,
but at least I know what they hold:

A toddler shouts "look" while spilling a
handful of chili beans down his shirt as
his mother rolls her eyes.
An old man whose vulnerability
finally catches up to him becomes
unable to wipe himself and stares
at his plumb shaped knees in the dark.
At ten years old I've sufficiently soaked
up the laughs of my friends, they come
tumbling out of me like a tape
recorder, syllables and magnetic
powder, congregating at the altar
of our intimacy. Sometimes, a cave
on the edge of a beach makes my
breathing shallow. Sometimes I
can't stop picking at my scalp and
arguing with the people in my mind.
It's all in there, it's all kinds, and I'll
keep reaching out my hand
toward these parts—
some belonging to you,
some belonging to me,
but I'll never question
if they're mine to touch.

Ode to Laziness

The yellow shelves I bought demanded
hammer and nail, two for two, and
on the evening I thought better
than to open the manual, I hung
them up with double sided industrial
tape. At midnight I awoke
to their jazz notes, plastic breaking
open under the weight
of my spices, walked in, saw the
basil, thyme, and parsley
littered in the shape of a circle
on my checkered floor:
a spell I dared
not disturb.

Spit It Out

He didn't come to say I'm sorry
meaning
he came to say I'm right
meaning
he came to say you're wrong
meaning
I'm wrong
meaning
I'm of wrath
meaning
my hands are bloodied
meaning
he died
meaning
I'm forgiven
meaning
I should be grateful
meaning
I'm off the hook
meaning
It's my fault if I find myself on the hook again
meaning
I'm not to be trusted
meaning
I'm a rotten vegetable
meaning
I can't pay these bills
meaning
I'm destitute
meaning
it's my fault
meaning

I have a good origin story
meaning
I'll have bad memories
meaning
I should talk to someone
meaning
I'm crazy
meaning
I'm a goner
meaning
I'm a waste of your time
meaning
let's talk later

What Is Sexier than Spring?

Everything is procreating
before our very eyes, not
(I like to think),
out of duty, or habit, or
dare I say, pleasure,
but out of the dripping
mouth from which
we all have learned to
speak, a language rarely
heard, a language
always seen.

I Digress

A morning spent as a body on the balcony;
exterior of linen, interior of disarray,
and I look up expecting
my right brain's lover,
my eyebrows in position to receive them.
Instead,
the air, or, rather, the earth, hands me a hummingbird.
And here I am
nose to nose
with what can only be described as
time in flight.
This body,
and my body,
two electricities
suspended in their own ways,
born into motion, dying—who can say when?
I used to believe it was a curse, the unknowing,
but the burden of knowing is not so unlike it.
I pause to breathe out,
I pause to be with this creature,
and a minute from now
I'm sure I'll regress back to that hidden hole of despair,
but, just for right now,
I know the sound of a good thing
humming above me.

Missive

I hadn't written a poem about you yet
and I told myself to write a poem about you yet
and the room was dark and it was just me there
until I told myself to write a poem about you yet
and we were counting the ducks on your sweater
and giving names to the men on your family tree
until I told myself to write a poem about you yet
and my teeth were stinging with the taste of you
and my toes were scrunching with the movement of you
until I told myself to write a poem about you yet
and I was sitting up after two hours in the back of the van
and you were finding your phone between the seats
until I told myself to write a poem about you yet

Flat Earther

In search of the perfect sky
I looked beyond the meditating waters,
lapping like blind dogs at my feet.

Famished and well-intentioned,
I searched and searched
for my prized morel
beneath the salmonberry bushes.

Just the other morning,
I juiced five oranges
as the fatty milk curdled
in its carton. I rejected
the sunny day's advances
for a chance to rest
in your arms. In the evening
I went so far as to trade
the constellations
for your breath.

While my love for you
outweighs all the scales,
it's time you knew:
my hands are porous,
my heart a sieve,
and in them
I've drained the world.

I've left so much behind me
while trying to run past
the horizon.

I'm always forgetting
the earth is round.

An Attempt

Lightning will not conform to you
like you hope she will.
Unlike water,
who takes the shape of
every vessel without protest,
this gift from above refuses to remain.
Though you have invited her in,
with your wit and your charm and your
many hours standing still in the muddied field,
she will refuse to live in the house of your body.
She will not overstay her welcome.
This is wishful thinking,
this is legend,
this is you trying to make the best of things
again.

And You Just Might

Put your fear
dead center
in your left palm.
Say the prayer
say the incantation
say the magic word
that translates to
help me.

And you just might
put your ear
to the door of heaven
arm outstretched
holding
    pain
        loneliness
            trembling madness
and hear
in the softest voice
you've ever touched
no.

And I hope
you find the will
to weep
from sheer delight.

God,
I hope you weep.

Wartime

and isn't somewhere
a black bear nursing her cub
and isn't somewhere
a man confessing his deep love
and isn't somewhere
the sun raising its hands
and isn't somewhere
life pursuing itself
even unto death

Urgent Relics

Let me see you living
in your body
as though it were a lasting thing

The Waiting Game

I live alone.
And when I dirty my dishes,
I don't wash them right away
because I like the idea of an
imperfect thing waiting for me
when I get home.

There, they'll sit stinking,
making conversation with the stovetop
and cutlery. The leather couch will hum along
with the refrigerator to pass the time, and the
untrimmed wicks will speak only to
say how intent they are upon my touch.

Many times I have bargained with God—
if I cannot have love, then let me at
least have presence. And if I cannot
have presence, then allow the absence to
speak.

One of Them

People make many sovereign attempts
to put their pain in the backseat
and watch it from the rear view.
It's okay to do this.
It's okay if you're one of them:
twenty four and hunched
over the toilet bowl puking
up sangria on family
vacation. You were made to
empty yourself anyway.

For so long you thought you knew
how to make this world better. For
so long you wanted to know who
you were.

It's okay
if after years of searching you finally
find yourself wet and skulking in
that plumbing: a squirmy gasping fish,
no bigger than your arm.
What a good catch
you think for a moment,
only to toss her back for fear
she'll drown upon taking her first
breath.

The Well

What goes on in me is none of your business,
but if you must to know:
in the morning I get up
only to lay back down
and stare at the ceiling until bees appear.
I spend all my time wondering if these hours will add up to anything.
I know what holds me together, and I know it isn't favorable.
Mostly, I'm tired of the world telling me I have a wound
when I know it to be a well,
and from it I pull water.

Part III

So we crawl
like babies are
known to do.
Accepting our
infancy as the only
part of us we really
need. Yes,
we crawl like babies
all different and
squeaky, some of us
faster than others.
We step on noses,
crunch hair in our
mouths, giggling.
We trade our
inheritances for snot
and cement.

Dating App Cento

Hey.
How are you?
Looks as though we may be intertwined.
Are you going to apologize?
If you're looking for something to scratch your itch,
Ruin me, please.
Respectfully, I mean.

How long has your week been?
Surviving the heat, groovy gal?
Luckily we have AC.
Omg your arm piece is incredible.
What's your tat meaning?
I have a Roma lady on my arm that I like.
What did the philosophical dog always wonder?
Am I ugly?

Did you know the platypus doesn't have a stomach?
Yes, and it is terrible.
Would my knowledge of Mitch Hedberg jokes I've memorized impress you?
Wanna smooch?
Wish I was at the river with you.
The photo in the snow is the cutest thing ever.
Who's your favorite comedian?
I suppose my favorite would be Kentaro Miura, Creator of Berserk.

Gorgeous.
Beautiful.
Lil Mama.
Cutie with the pretty eyes.
Ahh damn, you're such a babe.
I've been waiting for you mofo.

I mean, Descartes had a point
you are HOT,
and Descartes definitely got mad bitches.

I mostly embroider things and make rings and pendants.
I'm glad you have people to spend thanksgiving with.
I've read Toni Morrison recently and really like her.
I'm East Coast trash through and through.
Tell me the story from the first time you smoked weed.
I want to see a new part of the country soon.
The whole place smells like sage.
You a big dancer?

It makes sense—easier to qualify measurable vs emotional—but it's such a lack.
Just been being domestic with the kids and working on a woodworking project.
Do you have a favorite book?
"Demons" by Fyodor Dostoevsky and every now
and then I get through a few more pages of "War and Peace."
My grandma on my dad's side was named Rose
and my grandma on my mom's side's favorite flowers were daisies.
Yes, I love beer!

I felt blessed that there was almost no rain.
I need to step my candle game up.
What's your poison?
I want to downsize in 2021.
Let's get silly.

Oh my god, your anthem.
What do you like to get up to in the city?
Getting tangly is so nice with the right person.
Just like I used to do with the homies at sleepovers.
Sorry, that's all.
Forward, to the point.

He Couldn't Have

Every man once had the body of a boy,
thin as a lamppost and just as bright,
perhaps waiting for the train and
holding the hand of his mother each night.

Every boy once had the body of a baby,
thick as flour and just as light,
perhaps gawking at the lampshade
checkered thin in black and white.

Sensitivities

My mother says
she cannot be sensitive
when saying certain things
over breakfast.

Like the blue jay, she too
is plagued with aliveness and
is therefore fated to kill each morning.

Many times I have misunderstood
her nature, but when I write poems,
and write poems about poems, and
poems about the way the tiger lily's petals
look sharp as glass and just as clear,
how its pistils erect themselves like copper daggers
ready to spar while making love, and how desperately
I need to bear witness to what is beautiful
and what is ugly and what is true and far too often othered,
I realize I have equally as little patience for pleasantries
and just as much desire to say what can be cruel
but what is essential
with the same wet lungs that once grew
in her womb.

Love Poem

I washed my clothes
then hung them out to dry,
and, in between,
I thought of you,
before and after too.

Yes, It's Terminal

There are some words I refuse to write,
for fear it will confirm their frailty,
or worse,
their strength.

Right now I'm conducting the nightly visual ritual:
different parts of my body are melting into the ground, and
all I can see are my fingernails falling off,
my clit folding in on herself, as my head attempts rest on this pillow.

The mind is always chasing after what it can't catch;
a dumb dog running down the mail truck.

I try to remind myself
You haven't died yet, silly.
You can't know what it's like.
Don't worry, I'm too scared to off myself.

"My cowardice keeps me out of trouble,"
my old bible teacher used to say.
I agree, and still,
I want to stick my head out the window and scream
Don't you know we're all going to die? Me? You? Yes you! We're all terminally ill!
(I mean no disrespect to the terminally ill)

Last week on a beautiful beach I told my dearest friend I've sprung a leak,
and that soon all my bad parts will be oozing out everywhere.
She looked me in the eye and said 'Well, we're all doing that.'

So, in the mornings I tell myself I'm actually just a pillow filled with feathers.
Occasionally, a vase overflowing with oil.
I walk to my car and see a trail of innards behind me

and hope it doesn't scare my neighbors.
And every time it rains,
I shoot the sky a wink.

Oranges Are Earrings

I return from the funeral
fighting off the urge to wish
the whole world of my world of my world
had died
along with you.
If only to get this grief gone,
this grief I'm sitting next to gone,
that grief I'll meet again in four or forty years,
all at once,
gone.
Just fell swoop,
one big hug goodbye,
gone.
But that wouldn't be fair to you.

Cold Honey

a twinge follows after the break of a nickel sized snail shell
so stark it makes you question why we are born questioning
something so fundamental like watching your tooth fall out bloody and shining
knowing you've still lost something however small
knowing it will return to you doesn't quench your
confusion some things happen so snappily we pretend like
we chose between them to keep the blanket over us a little longer
and the saliva that moves upward against
the sides of our jaws is no match for the blue stars
oh say can i see them after driving for miles into the eyebrow of the sun
only able to see white when my eyes are open and blue stars
when they are closed, red and white, snail and tooth i don't ask
anymore why we sing these songs together and why
we are silent by ourselves because i should know by now to quit
my questions to accept them as what they pretend to be
because enough pretending can turn anything into anything and anyway
our voices were meant to bleed together

Figures

Ten years ago I had four parents,
now barely two.
What do I make of an excess
souring to absence, the kind
of choking which leaves me blue?

Counting the Unfinished Things

One. Lemon soup sitting on the left top burner
Two. Laundry pile by my bed, in an arrangement so uncanny it's almost talking
Three. Pink dinner candles dripping avalanches of wax, flame by flame
Four. My left knuckle out on a bender refusing to crack
Five. An argument
Six. A sincere apology (to and from)
Seven. My self imposed self actualization
Eight. A taped up photograph unsticking itself as we speak
Nine. Three prayers I recited last week
Ten. A cult documentary plastered on the living room TV paused intentionally so no
    one sees the carnage
Eleven. The wine at my bedside
Twelve. A copy of the book you lent me buried in the basement of my purse
Thirteen. My life, I pray
Fourteen. Our lives

I'll Miss My Disgust the Most

I'll miss nail biting,
sometimes swallowing,
before I stopped because I read that article about the man who couldn't shit
    anymore because of his nail ulcer.

I'll miss tattoos bleeding under their seranwraps,
first pink then out into the clear.

I'll miss the compost bin,
flowering with flies and
soon-to-be soil.

I'll miss my grandpa's body odor
and my father's sweaty back
running on a treadmill toward
nothing.

I'll miss this body's ability
to take in so much and
release toxins in trails
smelling like canned soup.

I'll miss blood streaked public
bathrooms the most—
one of the few
active catacombs left
that remind us
what we are.

On Mornings I Wish I Could Recite the Rosary

It is April, and you are here, and I am there.
Everything swells, and
I lay on my side with one hand open,
never knowing what to ask of God.
I settle on "encouragement" but it feels silly,
like a kiss from a man I barely know.

Apologizing to Roadkill

I'm sorry about before.
No one in your condition deserves such harsh words
and, in due time, someone will come along
and scoop you up, what you once were, and all that you will be.
They'll get almost every bit of you, maybe a little more than that too,
and, Roadkill, all I hope is
if you find no comfort, I pray you find peace, and
if you find no peace, I pray you find the eternal.

Ode to Dogwoods in April

because that is the flower's flower
isn't it? Cartoonish as it surprises
us year after year with our longing
for the landscape of its living,
asking, *can you believe we're both here?*
Declaring, *all you need is just one*
sniff to prove I'm not 2D,
just one touch to prove
I'm not a pastel sketch,
just one moment of your time, please,
to prove the earth can and so often does
give of herself more than she
asks in return.

The Talk

They never told me about hunger,
how it will move between your skin
like a cold snake trying to find the heat of any sun.

They never told me about the moon,
how she'll watch everything you do,
her many mouths open, gasping, singing along
to make up for god, sitting next to her, gritting his teeth.

They never told me I'd finish the job after two hours of someone else trying.
They never told me I could finish.

They never told me about the eroticism of ice cream, talking before
    and after and during, the laughter that gets me close, how too often
    we will be afraid of our own scents.

They never told me how hands could touch my stomach and it would
    feel like love and I'd like it. They never told me love could feel like a scratching
    in my throat, a cough I just can't kick.

These lines are the last fingers I'll point,
they can't say I never told them.

Pretty Little Thing

I wish I could crash the party
where my grandparents met,
smoke a little weed with them,
and fall asleep in the grass.

I can't.

So tell me again how the story goes—
late nights and the fish
dying, swirling in their tank
when you saw her,
minutes before you plucked her from the vine.

She never said it, but I knew:
sometimes, a cynical woman
needs a simple man to calm
her nerves. Sometimes, we
can't think too hard about
the people we love because
it might get in the way of
loving them.

Translations

Of course, there is the fear.
When the animal you've come to know
as your body no longer stands upright
below the one sun that grew it.
Of course, there is the fear.

But of what?
We breathe in the night more deeply than the morning.
Of course, there is the fear.

And all the birds know it too,
and they still feast,
and they still fly.
Of course, there is the fear.

As you walk, your ankles smile into the ground.
If you look closely you can see pearled teeth below the bone.

When you speak a new language for the first time,
of course, there is the fear.

Birth Work

Oh to know
what it's like to hold
something wet and bright and struggling

I Was Making Lemon Cake

I was making lemon cake.
It was going great
until I saw Bob Saget was laid to rest,
and I couldn't bring myself to read the articles.
The headlines were enough for me.

I was making lemon cake.
I never watched Full House,
maybe caught a couple episodes one time.
Cultural icon,
Bob Saget was a dirty comedian, right?
That's what someone told me once.

I was making lemon cake.
I never knew the man.
My fingers dripped juice, zest, flakey salt.
Bob Saget.
Who has a last name like that?

I was making lemon cake.
Ten years ago had I heard this
I would have stood in the kitchen
whispering prayers for a man I never knew and hardly knew of.
"Lord, have mercy on Bob."

I was making lemon cake.
No,
I wouldn't have said it like that.
How would it have gone?
"Lord, comfort Bob's friends and family and bring him to you."
Is there any way to be sure of what we once asked of God?

I was making lemon cake.
That seems wrong too.
Perhaps I wouldn't have said the words.
Perhaps I would have felt a thump in my chest
    and would have known he got the message.

I was making lemon cake.
Perhaps that's what I'm doing now.

Thief

We could imitate these actions,
skin the characters, clean them
and dress them, sew their faces
onto our faces,

it wouldn't be romantic,
don't go getting any ideas,
but it would be a spectacle,
and, anyway,
what wouldn't you sacrifice
if you could resurrect yourself
on the altar of someone else's
mistakes?

Part IV

We writhe,
we writhe,
until it's time.
The draining
ducts open
one by one.
We fumble around
for hands to hold,
everyone squeezing
so tightly
the nails leave
crescent moons
to carry in our palms.
The draining begins and
we cry openly,
we cry witnessing,
we cry to be witnessed,
some of us for the last time.

Last Night I Masturbated to the Memories of My Embarrassments

One by one they run, across
the streets of my mind
marked by the pear
trees, knowing
I was watching.

Their bodies? Vast.
Their strong will? Resisting every plead of a final
form.
Their eyes? Seducing me with the fullness
of all the things that had happened
and of all the things that hadn't
and of all that finally brought me to myself.

What if I loved them?
What if I loved them?

E Major

For Ellie

You speak to me,
and it sounds like you're reciting the
living poem.
Something you said
a long string
of years ago.
Something, perhaps,
you yelled when you were six
or babbled when you were three.

I used to be afraid
I wasn't worth your newness,
but now I know
when we talk
it's like how we were
at the beginning:
when everything was radiant
and moving over the waters
and togetherness was a given.

After Hours

I want to be reverent of all the good things and bow so low when I am told.

Knees shaking so holily, the candle wax dripping on my shoulder blades
as I recite everything I know
about the origin of earth, wine, and God.

So many analogies for sex in the Bible, how do we choose?
Every preacher I know would blush
or pound his fist on the pulpit if he read them twice.

So many metaphors for intimacy.
They pile on top of one another between us and I never get to touch you.

My ring burns hot! I sweat it right off.

Solomon had hundreds of wives!
How did he pick a favorite?
I'm all but sure it was the one who knew
to put honey on wounds and balance water on her breasts.
Make young men drink.
Make them forget to think.

I want to be reverent of all the good things, but my hands are bleeding again.
My head is bowed to hide.

Could this be as simple as doing as the old ones did?

Come with me
and find shelter within
a thousand blue trees.
Say yes.

Remember the good thing
has always belonged to you.

I Ask the Wind

Hello wind
Hello you

I know you
As well as I know you

Then you know why I have come
I do not know you *that* well

But you know what man has done and who it is he who levels the earth
I do know

And you know what man has done and who tells the pregnant stars to begin showing
I do know

And you, who have no beginning and no end, no mother and no father,
    have seen the dividing lines
I have seen

And to whom do you answer?
I have only myself

What is it like to answer only to yourself?
It is like being free

What is freedom?

Survival Tactics

For Castine

The belly of my friend is swollen
under my hands as we sit on the porch
and wonder aloud about what her
daughter will look like in a couple
of months.

After years of starving her body,
my friend is finally full.
She has met herself
twice over and likes what she sees.

She is blinking in the light. She is
very beautiful and still on this Sunday morning.
She is alive and I have been a witness to her living.

What more can I ask of God?

Dying Day

Sometimes when you cross your fingers I think you're praying
and not just to me or to the mailman who, god love him, brings us
Sherdy's porno subscriptions instead of the daily (just bring us
our daily),

but had we never moved to this city I would never have thought
to cross my legs, or, better yet, I'd pull the rare and formidable
ankle cross to get the attention of my own deity (finally!)
who in turn calls me after the knife show has already started (rude!),

and one more question—do tea leaves have the same effect if
I cut open the bag after I've drained my cup or what if I make
a trail to the bedroom for someone to follow, not you, you're
palling with Sherdy, (don't we know it),

and I don't give you
enough credit

Lord help me, I need to start thinking better of
my wrinkled knuckles and the baby blue baby sky, baby, it's
just that the towers fell quick like that ugly giant Rev is always on
about and this is my final warning
(oh please, I've been trying to tell ya!):

it's my turn to fall down now.

Dear Tony Robbins,

There is no final form.

Thank You

the universe hates the word time,
but she loves the word slow. before
you curse her, remember the gifts—
your first bedroom, your mother's womb
before you knew walls should be painted,
but if you could paint a womb
what would yours have looked like?
would you have painted flowers or sail boats or even, a window?

more gifts now, the way you can walk in time
to the sounds around you, the many gifts of sound,
how in your dream last night the morning bird found you
and you dreamt her song was a warning,
how warnings are just another way your body tells you it cares
and is happy you are alive.

the gift of laying down with your legs crossed over one another,
the warmth that can be found with yourself, not in spite of another,
     but because you were born alone and you will leave alone and that's nothing to grieve
over.

and look! my hands have shelves to rest in:
built in ones laid bare on the sides of my hips
open, and deserving of every gentle yes,
there's nowhere you need to be but here,
isn't that terrifying? isn't that a reason to say
thank you?

No Miracles in March

Moonlight makes me
achey, and taxes do frighten,
and you plead with me
a third time to consider
the spirits. Forgotten drops
of spring rain come
too quickly, then not
at all, lovingly replaced
by beads of sweat on your back
soaking into my sheets.
    We could die at any moment,
      and I have made my mistakes,
and there you are—
smiling in my kitchen
while the sun bleeds into our scene,
so casual like as we both pretend
this is just something that happens,
maybe it happens all the time, as
we tell ourselves
this is no miracle.

Venus

I don't want a daughter.
I want a word.
One that will spell the story of me correctly.
One that will abandon me quickly so I don't have to wait around.

I don't want a son.
I want a brick.
One that won't break me.
One that will help me build my first and only wall.

In harder years, they made me out to be a poison in the hands of one man.
They made me out to *be* man, deformed.
They called me arrogant and boundless,
like their favorite flavor of cancer.

And who is this portion of light
come to rescue me from my selfishness
and scattered devotions?
It is no matter.

On more than one occasion,
I will find him shivering
between two tomorrows,
begging to eat the scraps off
my table,
begging for his only chance
to become something
weighted.

Codependence

You elaborate me
as I elaborate you
within these fleshed-out corridors
of this well-intentioned heart
we must destroy

Small Bodies

You can
die for it—
an idea
a word
a world.

People
have done so,
phenomenally,
letting
their small bodies
be bound
to the stake—
creating the infinite,
when they believed
they were dying for it.

Little Christ

Put him in your pocket, he'll fit just right.
Clip him to your hijab he'll do just fine.
Sit with him on the bus, I know he'll pay your fare.
Follow him to the penitentiary, he'll meet you on a dare.
Hand him a toothpick and some ink to write his name.
Just don't be surprised when it never sounds the same.

To Uncover, To Reveal

There is no word like apocalypse to get people baking again;
to get the women standing, knees bent in, mixing the oatmeal,
palm feeding their children, sinking back into an honest day's work.
No one word like it that will see the men hang their hats on the
dusty peg and finally tell their mistresses off, one word to see
the graduates fold their gowns. There is no setting
like the present (although we don't know this to be sure) to steer
the masthead of youth away from learning toward some other,
"marvelous" virtue.

In the olden days of plague they turned to the sky,
now we turn toward one another. Rubbing eyeballs. Bumping chins.
Trying to fit back together in the way we never did.
The musicians press pause, the dancers stand still.
The poets pick up their pens only to drop them on the linoleum.
We call our mothers, we yell at our fathers,
until she picks up the spoon and begins to stir again.

The East

What was I to do
when the popcorn ceiling dropped down on the both of us
like the glass is dropping now?

You're fumbling for my fingers
as if that will save us from revelation,
but there is no Hail Mary left,
not in my bones or my blood,
though I can still hear her singing.

You find what you've been looking for, but I turn to the left,

straightening the curves in my ribs where you nested yourself
time after time
in a fury of intelligent, interior design.

Yes, I turn to the left,
toward The East where the sun promises to rise and men are kinder.

I turn to the left,
toward one more unreachable thing.

A House

When you die, instead
of sinking, expand:
into a house,
wood floorboards and all,
and write the love
we've said to each other
on the mirror
so I can speak
to you
still.
I won't ring the bell,
just walk inside:
your roof will
keep me dry,
your kitchen cupboards
have more than I need,
your windows will
teach me how to see
the world rightly,
again.

The Complete Portrait of Human Nature

Someone I loved told me they loved me.
It is almost enough to convince me I am good.

The Buck Moon

On the night of the Buck Moon
we went to witness
the shyness and the sovereignty
of that great place
many believe we conquered,
knowing full well
she visited us first.

All of us admitted
none of us knew when or where,
but we watched
the mountain peak begin to glow
and waited patiently
for the miracle.

And when she rose,
You turned to me and said,
"Now I can see your face."

Bath, North Carolina

Southern towns, quiet quiet, all
hushed under the weight
of this sweet and heavy air.

Dylan, only four, jumps
from stone to stone and
lays his body down on a large
square burial plot, extending
his arms to feel the cool
memorial stone hold him
up from the ground.

Do some bodies remember
what we have yet to do?

Let's keep going, he says.

Speaking Grief

these days I speak only in glow stick
fragments, no connector between them.
i speak in lowercase,
and loudly sometimes, but quiet always.
i speak from the gurgles of my belly,
a tapped foot, skin picking other skin.
i have spoken all my life
only to discover
the voice is not the life.
the words are a singing companion.
beside me lays a life.

Reverse Pareidolia

Like when my brother's gray jacket looked like an elephant hanging on its peg but barely: the one he took the day you passed away. Too small for his shoulders we all thought at first, but then it grew into him and we couldn't object.

Objects, like people, can belong to anyone and do. The hands that hold them may change, the wearers and the movers. Like the infant who doesn't know where his mother begins after her breast, the things we belong to can't help but belong to us.

The Irrational Woman

In another life I do not do the things I am doing.
I am not pouring the steamed milk
on top of your cup as though it were some sacred act,
bringing it to you with my hands folded over in prayer.
I would not pretend to be gorgeous
nor act as though I was good.
I would not be laughing with you under the chestnut tree,
collecting our blessings in the grass.
Memory is made of two ingredients: time and hope.
If I could hope for anything right now,
I'd like to be clean and dead, staring down
atop a wide hill, watching
you remember me.

ACKNOWLEDGMENTS

Thank you to my mother and father for showing me early on in my life what it means to be a steward of language, each in their own way. Thank you to my publisher and friend Keith Giles for seeing something in my work and fanning the flame. Thank you to my lifelong friends, family, and mentors, particularly Marlys Samler, Castine Friberg, and Ray Poklacki, for holding onto me through so many years and never letting go. Thank you to Richard Marymee for teaching me many things, but most overwhelmingly, that reconciliation and forgiveness are the whole damn point of being here; and thank you for giving me reasons to miss you. Thank you to my beautiful community in Portland, you have forever changed me. Thank you to foolishness and embarrassment for your immeasurability and your lifeblood, I'm beginning to enjoy your company. Finally, thank you to the whistling divinity who accompanies me on my walks, visits me in my dreams, and loves me in the depths of my shadows—you've been there from the beginning, and you'll be there at the end, and you're living in these poems, and I'm grateful.

To contact Hannah Dulaney for speaking engagements,
please email hannahdulaney@gmail.com.

Many Voices. One Message.

quoir.com